EXPLAINING
What the Bible says about Work

DAVID PAWSON

ANCHOR RECORDINGS

Copyright © 2016 David Pawson

The right of David Pawson to be identified as author of this Work has been asserted by him in accordance with the Copyright, Designs and Patents Act 1988.

First published in Great Britain in 2016 by
Anchor Recordings Ltd
Synegis House, 21 Crockhamwell Road,
Woodley, Reading RG5 3LE

No part of this publication may be reproduced or transmitted in any form or by any means, electronic or mechanical, including photocopy, recording or any information storage and retrieval system, without prior permission in writing from the publisher.

**For more of David Pawson's teaching,
including DVDs and CDs, go to
www.davidpawson.com**

**FOR FREE DOWNLOADS
www.davidpawson.org**

**For further information,
email: info@davidpawsonministry.com**

ISBN 978-1-911173-36-6

Printed by Lightning Source

This booklet is based on a talk. Originating as it does from the spoken word, its style will be found by many readers to be somewhat different from my usual written style. It is hoped that this will not detract from the substance of the biblical teaching found here.

As always, I ask the reader to compare everything I say or write with what is written in the Bible and, if at any point a conflict is found, always to rely upon the clear teaching of scripture.

David Pawson

EXPLAINING
What the Bible says about Work

It is very rarely thought about that we spend something like fifty percent of our lives in work. While we are at work we are spending sixty percent of the time we are awake at work. The tragedy is that so much of that is being wasted and kept from the kingdom by those who work, because Christianity has become a leisure time activity and God never intended that. So I want to tell you about the Christian doctrine of work – however unpopular it may be. Do you imagine that an ideal world would be a world without work? That is not God's ideal at all.

How do you think of heaven? According to many preachers I have listened to it appears to be going to be an everlasting Sunday morning service where every chorus is sung seventeen million times! Frankly, if that is heaven I am not really looking forward to it! But it is how many preachers assume it will be – especially song leaders assume it's going to be – and that they are the ones who are really going to be in full-time service there.

For many, even Christians, work is a necessary evil and if they could do without it they would. Why do you think lotteries are so popular? We have a national lottery in England now and tickets are sold to many every day, though their chances of winning are so low – infinitesimal. But why are they doing it? Because they are hoping to get out of work, and that is the one chance most people will have of stopping work. Then there are those who are looking forward to early retirement, and therefore being able to choose what they do as early as possible, spending the rest of their lives doing what they want to do.

There are two extreme attitudes to work. One I call "the idolatry of work" and the other I call "the immorality of work", and idolatry and immorality are the two great distractions from God's work in scripture. The idolatry of work is to be a workaholic, to make your work the biggest thing in your life, to go for promotion, to live for it, to do as much in it as you can. Such people don't look forward to retirement. Indeed, many of them retire and die quite quickly. They have lived for their work – it is their idol. But that is an extreme, I admit. The other extreme is more common. What is the immorality of the workplace? Quite simply, to do as little work as you can for as much money as you can. That is usually the cry of a trade union in England, "We are striking for shorter hours and more pay." If we can cut down on work and increase our money, that is the objective. That is actually immoral. But it is sometimes practised at the workplace by a thing which I learned to call "skiving". That word was coined when I was a Chaplain in the Royal Air Force. I think it means to appear to be working when you are not, and it is a highly skilled activity. You appear to be rushing around the office and seem to be very busy, but you are not at all. You are really only interested in the pay packet. So, when the boss is looking, you are working jolly hard, and when he looks away you can relax and catch up with your friends on your mobile phone.

So there is an idolatry of work and an immorality of work. Most people are somewhere in between the two. But a Christian is quite different in work. Do you know, in my country there is more sickness on Mondays and Fridays than any other day of the week? A majority of people report in sick or send a report in that they are sick on Mondays and Fridays – which means a longer weekend. People can spend their leisure time in such a way that they are less fit for work. They are not "recreated" for work, they haven't engaged in recreation. They have engaged in an exhausting time when they have been on their own and therefore appear late on Monday morning. I am sure you know what I am referring to, but I am addressing Christians so I am talking to people who never do that! Do you think there will be work in heaven? I think so.

Actually, we were made for work. God put us on the earth for work, and that is where I want to begin. What I am really saying is that we have been profoundly influenced by Greek culture – maybe without realising it. Our educational system is basically Greek. Our architecture, until the days of steel and reinforced concrete and glass, was largely Greek. Most public buildings up to the middle of the twentieth century look like Greek temples with Corinthian columns and plaster above. But the Greeks lived for leisure. Their whole life was geared around leisure. The ambition of every Greek man was to be a gentleman of leisure. They solved this problem by getting all the manual labour done by slaves, and most of their slaves – who formed two-thirds of the population – had been bought. Not brought but *bought* in from foreign countries.

Now take Europe, for example. Much of the manual labour is being done by foreigners to Europe. The "Greek" ambition was to get others to do your hard work, and you can be a person of leisure who can go to the theatre, who can debate in the forum, who can be a gentleman of culture – and culture was largely a leisure activity.

The technological age is doing a lot of different things to that. The industrial revolution favoured men rather than women. The industrial revolution needed hands – strong hands, factory hands. The technological revolution is favouring women. They have neater fingers to touch little buttons on machines, and in fact that has introduced a lot of employment for women.

Should Christians work if they can avoid it? And if they do work, how can that work be claimed for the kingdom of God so that it is not just, "I serve the kingdom of God in my leisure time"? Every Christian discipleship course, I have discovered, is based on the assumption you can only be a Christian in your leisure time – not one has mentioned work. It is: how to pray; how to evangelise; how to spend time with the Word; what you should do; it is about church. When you go through all the Christian discipleship things you have to do, you need to have a lot of leisure time, because that is when all those things are done!

Again, it has thrown away the majority of your life. I want you to realise that your work is the biggest thing you can do for the kingdom of heaven, because it takes most of your time and it can be part of the kingdom of God. The Bible says a great deal about work – a lot that is rather embarrassing. It tells all Christians to earn their living. Now that doesn't rule out receiving gifts or legacies, but it tells us that earning money is part of being a Christian. Frankly, that means getting your money from those who benefit from your labour. That is my definition of earning. That is legitimate income.

I am disturbed by the number of young people whose ambition it is to live off relatives, and by raising money so that they can go and be a missionary or do some full-time work. I have pointed out elsewhere that Jesus, the Son of God, who was called to be the Saviour of the world, spent eighteen years first working for a living with his hands. Incidentally, the Bible tells you that it is the healthiest form of work – to work with your hands rather than your head. If your daily labour does not involve your hands then I believe you should find a leisure activity that does, to balance up.

People who work with their hands are conspicuous for not needing psychiatrists. Think of a gardener who is working with his hands all the time and producing plants – very rarely do they have a nervous breakdown. All the great people of the Bible prepared by working with their hands. Paul, the greatest missionary there has been, was a tent-maker and spent a lot of his time sewing canvas. You think: what a waste of a man like Paul, with his intellect, vision and energy. He did it because he voluntarily wanted to give an example to his converts. He tells them that, "I laboured among you with my hands so that you might have an example to follow." Amazing!

We are going to look at the biblical example of work and what the Bible actually says. My teaching will be divided into three parts headed "Creation", "Fall" and "Redemption", because those three are the phases of most doctrines in the Bible: what God intended in Creation, what happened when the human race fell into sin, and how this can be redeemed through Christ.

So let us start right at the beginning with Creation. God is a worker, a manual labourer; he works with his hands. God hasn't got physical hands, he hasn't got physical eyes or ears or arms or legs or feet. Yet the Bible talks about all those things – it even talks about his bowels. Yet he hasn't got any. He is not a physical being, he is Spirit. But it does clearly mean that he has functions in his Spirit that are equivalent to the functions in our body. So we have eyes, God can see. We have a nose that we can smell with, and it says God smells.

I know of a little boy who was in school having a biology lesson and he was crying and the teacher said, "What's the matter?" He replied, "God's made me all wrong. It's my feet that smell and my nose that runs." But every physical attribute you have and use, God has anyway. You are made in his image, even physically. His functions are reflected in your organs and senses. So the Bible is quite legitimate in what the scholars call "anthropomorphism" – a horrible word, but it means you can talk about God as if he is in human form, though you must remember that he is not: you can see, he can see; you can hear, he can hear; you can touch, he can touch; you have hands, he has hands; you have arms, he has arms, and so it goes on. Since your bowels are the seat of your compassion in Hebrew physiology, it talks even of the "bowels" of God.

Every part of us corresponds to a function of God. In that amazing way, when you read that he made you in his image, don't rule out your physical body. That too is in his image. So God is portrayed as a worker. Therefore he took a day off after six days' work and he exists apart from his work and his work is not his life. It is a major part, and therefore the creation around us is always called in the Bible his "handiwork". That is why Jesus came and said, "My Father works until now, and now I work." That is as true of his eighteen years as a carpenter as of his three years in public ministry. He was giving us a picture of God.

That is beginning at the creation. He put man on the earth to fill it with people, to subdue it to his own purposes and to look after it. "Adam was a gardener, and God who made him sees that every proper gardener's work is done upon his knees," goes the old poem. But his work was as a gardener. It was therefore suited to him, it was good for him, it was healthy, it was not exhausting.

By the way, the Garden of Eden has been discovered. You can now go and see it. It was discovered by an Egyptologist who is not a Christian. He is a very gracious, charming man and has now discovered for himself that the Old Testament is historically and geographically accurate. His name is David Rohl and he has produced two coffee table books on his work, one of which is called *A Test of Time*. He has made some amazing discoveries in Egypt. He has discovered Joseph's house and tomb and a statue of Joseph in the land of Goshen. It is very exciting. His work was on BBC television in a most impressive series. He has even found why there were seven years of famine after seven years of plenty. The famine was not due to lack of water but too much. The Nile flooded and its banks – which are normally flooded once a year with sediment and moisture – were flooded right through the year and no crops could grow for seven years. He has found the ruins of huge storehouses of grain near the upper Nile where all the food was stored during the seven fat years. He has even found a canal from the Nile to a great depression in the Saharan desert where water was run off from the Nile in the good years to provide a reservoir of water. It is still to this day called by the Arabs "Joseph's Canal". All this is very exciting. But then, as an Egyptologist, he discovered the name of Israel in hieroglyphics for the first time in Egypt.

He has now taken it further back from the time of Joseph – right back to Eden. He believed there were enough geographical details in Genesis 2 to help him, and he found it. I will describe it for you. It is a valley about fifty miles long, surrounded by very tall mountains that shut it in. It is a beautiful valley, sloping down to a lake at the bottom, which is nearly a hundred miles long and perhaps twenty miles wide. The thing which is most exciting is that it is a valley that is still full of fruit trees because the climate in that valley is just perfect for growing fruit. There it is – quite isolated.

But there are passes in the valley, into the land of Nod at the east, which is exactly where Genesis says it was. The four rivers that are mentioned all find their sources near this valley. If you want to find it on the map, the second biggest town of Iran is there and it is called Tabriz. So if you look up

Tabriz in your atlas then you have found the Garden of Eden and you will see in a physical atlas the exact description I have given you, which is the one place that fits Genesis 3.

I hope you are as excited as I am about this – that a man who is not even a believer is convinced every word in the Old Testament is historically accurate. He has no axe to grind; he is not trying to prove anything. That is rather different from a Christian who has a built-in motive to find confirmation of the truth of the Bible. But that was where God put Adam, and he said, "Now you are to be a gardener, you are to till the ground, you are to look after the trees." The primary task would be pruning, picking fruit, and what I would call congenial labour. But as soon as the Fall came, of course, that all changed.

Now from this beginning we can deduce certain things very clearly. First of all, in the Creation which God called good – and, when he made man, very good – there was work and indeed a *duty* to work. By the way, Adam didn't have a Sabbath. We often think he did because we are told about the Sabbath rest of God in the same chapters as we are told about Adam, but Adam was never told to have recreational rest. As far as we know he could have worked seven days a week. Abraham didn't have a Sabbath, Isaac didn't, Jacob didn't. The Sabbath rest of one day a week was introduced by Moses. That is why you will find the Sabbath law under the Mosaic covenant. That is when it was introduced – in a covenant that was temporary until Christ came. The Sabbath rest of the New Testament is quite different from the one day a week (read Hebrews 4). But Adam, in this congenial labour, laboured (as far as we know) every day, and spent the evening with God at the end of the day, talking over the day no doubt – talking over many things. But in the cool of the evening was his time with God and his rest. We know that every evening he had that fellowship with his Creator.

We have the anthropomorphic description of God taking a walk in the garden each evening. The Bible is all very real and down to earth. So the first thing we deduce from all this is this: Eden was not a holiday camp. It was a place of work for gardening. Adam was a tenant and was to work for God there and look after it. It is now a much more ordinary valley. It has still got the fruit trees but now it has got that great town of Tabriz slapped in the middle of it. But you can still get away from the town quite quickly and see Eden nearly as it was – not quite, in fact there are two trees missing from it: the Tree of Life and the Tree of Knowledge. But otherwise it is reasonably like it used to be.

The second deduction I want to make concerns the *dignity* of work and, above all, the dignity of manual work. For Adam worked with his hands not his head. Man was made in the dignity of his Creator, and working with your hands is not to be despised. But in most human societies manual workers are at the bottom of the pile and people want to get away from that into white-collar work, piloting a desk, for some reason. Never despise manual labour. Jesus was eighteen years doing it. Paul was a tent-maker. King David was a shepherd, learning to use a sling and a crook. Manual labour has dignity and is not the lowest type of work. I even tend to think it is the highest in God's sight, but I'll leave you to agree or disagree with that.

Thirdly, work was intended to be a *delight*, not a hard, suffocating thing that caused strain and stress, but something that would bring fulfilment, satisfaction. In fact, when you do something with your hands that is very satisfying. I love doing something with my hands – building, carpentry. But the thing is that when you have done something with your hands, the pleasure of standing back and saying "I did that" is only surpassed by the greater pleasure of your wife saying: "What a wonderful husband I have – that he can make that."

In our last home I rebuilt and rebuilt, and moved around, and I did this and did that. The only downside is that anything practical that needs to be done – who is called to do it? Like every husband I have a list of things to be done in the house. I am afraid that the more you do, the longer it seems to get. But if you are good with your hands you will make a good husband for someone. Any time there is a leak somewhere or something has gone wrong, the wife can turn to the husband and say, "Fix it." When you have fixed it, the satisfaction comes – when you really have fixed it, and if you have difficulty fixing it, then it is misery.

Well now, the duty, the dignity, and the delight of work. Jesus came to show us what God is like, and therefore he showed us manual labour six times as long as serving the Lord directly by preaching and doing miracles.

Two negatives come from the Creation facts. One is: laziness is a sin in the Bible – idleness. The book of Proverbs says, "Go to the ant, thou sluggard, and study her ways." When you study ants they are always running about carrying burdens far bigger than themselves. They are workers and they work like Trojans. They are amazing little things. The book of Proverbs is full of proverbs against sloth, not working; against idleness. The damage that brings to the person as well as to others is clearly highlighted there. It is not a sin that is usually confessed in Roman Catholic confessional boxes, but it is one of the deadly sins in Catholic theology and they got it from the Bible. Laziness is a sin.

The second negative I draw from creation: unemployment is an evil. A Christian should fight it. Now you may live in a happy situation in a country where there are more jobs than people and where unemployment is incredibly low and you can easily find a job. It is not the way in Europe. In European countries unemployment is climbing, it is a major problem and some people spend all their life unemployed.

They may even have a university degree in our country and they have difficulty getting a job. That is devastating. When a man gets up in the morning and has nothing to work at, it is destructive.

Therefore Christians have a concern for the unemployed, not just to hand out food and money, but to get people a job. Unemployment is a social evil and therefore to be fought by Christians. I thank God that I have friends who are in a position to do so, whose contribution to the "Third World" is not to pour out money and aid, but to create jobs for them, to create employment. One of my closest friends is setting up thousands of people in India as taxi drivers by buying taxis and selling them bit by bit to drivers in India who work and gradually pay him back and finish up owning a taxi and in business. That is the best thing, I think, that can be done for those parts of the world where unemployment is rife.

Christians are doing it and are very concerned to provide the work that makes a man a man. Notice that I am talking about men. We are made differently, God made male and female. One of the basic differences between the genders is this: a man lives for a goal. He has to have something to go for. He has to get up in the morning and feel that there is something calling him to go further. A man lives for the future therefore, to establish something, to build something. Women are made differently. Now I make these differences relatively because there is a kind of overlap, and there are some male-type women and some female-type men. But the average male lives for the future and for a goal. The average female lives for a need. Since the world is so full of needs, a woman finds it easier to meet a need, if only to put the kettle on for a cup of tea. That is the instinctive reaction of a British woman to a crisis: she runs and puts the kettle on, anything that will help to meet a need. Since there are so many needs, a woman, even if she is not employed to do so, can find purpose in meeting the needs of others. But a man who is out of work feels useless, he feels unwanted; he feels that life is passing him by. I just mention that because unemployment hits a man much more than a woman for that reason.

But it is relative, as all differences between the genders are. So laziness is a sin and unemployment is an evil, and the Bible urges us about both. In fact, at one stage Paul taught this: "if any will not work, neither shall he eat." I once had a young man come to see me at twelve o'clock – and he came and sat down, which I did too. He was what I call a "professional student", and as soon as he finished one course he applied for another, and then another. He had already been nine years spending his life studying at the taxpayer's expense and felt no guilt, and didn't ever want a job. He was going to go on like that as long as he could. He was very persuasive and he was interviewed again and again for courses and they always accepted him.

So he came in. Now I said it was twelve o'clock and our sitting room and our dining room was one and the same (at different ends), and the table was set for lunch. I noticed that his eyes kept going to the table. I kept him talking. One o'clock came, half past one, two o'clock. Still I'm talking to him, and he's still looking at the dinner table – it's torture, really. Finally, he couldn't help but burst out with, "Are you having lunch shortly?" Then he admitted he had called at twelve o'clock because he had rather hoped to have lunch with us. I said, "Well, I'm very sorry, I can't invite you to lunch because the Bible forbids me to." He looked at me in absolute astonishment. He said, "Where?" I took him to that scripture: "If a man will not work, neither shall he eat." At that point he left in not a very good mood. That was that, and then we got on with our lunch.

A few weeks later the doorbell rang and here he was again

at the same time. I said, "Well?" He said, "You can give me lunch today." I asked him, "Why?" He replied, "Well, I've finished studies and I've taken a job." I said, "You can eat every bit of food in the house now – you're welcome to it all!" I was simply applying the Word of God. Yes, in a very blunt way, but he needed to learn that, and he did. Now he began to pay back the country for all the money that the country had spent on his leisure study. Was that being cruel or harsh? I don't believe so. The church should not be a soft touch for people who don't want to work. It doesn't say, "If a man *cannot* work he must not eat." If a man cannot work there is full liberty to help him. But it is "If a man will not" – and that is a serious situation.

Now in all this I am talking about *before* the Fall. So let's move into this second phase and look again at work. What happened to it when man got out of God's will – when Adam disobeyed God? We know how embarrassed he was that when God came for his evening walk he was hiding with his wife among the bushes. God asked him, "Adam, where are you?" God knew perfectly well where he was, he wanted Adam to confess where he was. Adam finally said, "We're over here in the bushes because we're naked and we're embarrassed." Interesting that that was the first effect of the Fall. But what happened to his work? Well, we know from the Bible. It is interesting when God's feelings are touched. Again I am using an anthropomorphic word there, but the Bible is full of God's feelings. I want to shout out to the world, "God has feelings too!" What I feel about God doesn't really matter, but what God feels about me matters greatly. Did you ever ask at the end of a day how God felt about your day? Was he happy with it? Was he sad, was he grieved, was he angry? You need to know about God's feelings. He has feelings. We are in his image and we have feelings, and therefore he has too.

God's feelings are expressed in scripture in poetry. His thoughts are expressed in prose. There is a big clue for understanding the Bible: when you read the Bible, notice when you change to poetry. I hope you have a translation of the Bible that sets out the poetry in short lines with gaps, and prose like a newspaper, column to column, because then you know when you are reading about God's feelings. In the early chapters of Genesis and the story of Adam and Eve, God has feelings too – so had Adam. When Adam first saw Eve he said, "Wow, that's really something," and he immediately expressed himself in poetry.

Do you know that seventy-five percent of all songs ever written have been love songs between men and women? Even pop songs – the great majority are about love between boy and girl. The first time Adam ever sang was when he saw Eve. Therefore from that song you can judge that he has got feelings, and who would blame him for that? Because every other animal God created had a mate and now he had a mate and he was happy. God spoke to Adam and Eve and the serpent. By the way, the serpent had legs until then, so it was not a snake, it was more a lizard.

By the way again, it wasn't an apple. It was fruit, and we don't know what kind of fruit it was. All these myths gather up around the truth and legends come in. But when Adam fell, God's punishment was to change his work. The poem which describes what happened to it is fascinating. His work was to become very much harder, he would now work in the sweat of his brow. He was going to plough the land now; he was changed from a gardener to a farmer. He would not only find that much harder, but he would be battling against weeds, against thorns and thistles. If you want to see the biggest thorns and thistles in the world go to the Middle East. Go to Israel and you will find thorns that are two to three inches long – terrible things. It makes you wonder what a crown of thorns would be like to wear. The thistles grow up to six feet tall and very thick, and it is hard work getting rid of those two things from your land, and you will have to get rid of them before you can plough it and get anything back to eat. This was the curse that God put on the ground as punishment for having left his will. Eve's punishment was in her relationships, both with her husband and with her babies.

The serpent's punishment was to lose his legs and to slither on the ground from then on. Do you know that every snake has legs? I didn't know that. I know a man who kept snakes in his garage as a hobby – the last thing I would ever do. He had great big snakes squirming around in his garage and he picked one up and wrapped it around his neck and then he said, "I'll show you something." About two-thirds of the way along its body he pries up the scales on his body, and lo and behold, underneath those scales were shrivelled little legs. I never knew that before, did you? The snake has legs but God's curse on the snake was to say: you will lose them and you will be an enemy of women now, and from now on.

Built into that was a prophecy that one day the seed of the woman would bruise his head, even while the serpent bruised his heel. It is the first prophecy which tells us that God knew right from the beginning how he would deal with this situation. But what happened to work? It became harder. It became more meaningless. It became his identity. All these things are now showing through work today: it is hard; it is often meaningless.

I went to an aircraft factory that was building V-bombers in Britain during the Cold War. There was a man there and he had a big machine in front of him and a lever. He would take a flat piece of aluminium and put it under this press, pull the lever down, lift it up again, and pass this piece of bent aluminium on to someone else. I was fascinated. I said,

"Is that all you do all day – week in, week out?" They didn't then change people's jobs to keep them interested. He had this job for years. What a boring job! I said, "What part does that piece of aluminium play in the ultimate aircraft?" He replied, "I don't know." I could tell that he wasn't even interested in what he was doing. But of course he was one of those who have the kind of job which is to get money, either to survive and keep the family or to be able to spend in leisure time. He had lost a purpose or meaning in what he was doing during the day. It wasn't entirely his fault, but at least he could have said, "I'm making part of the cabin of a V-bomber" and had an interest in what he was doing. But he had lost all that and I really felt sorry for him.

So it has become hard, it has become meaningless and it is becoming our identity. If you ask me what I am, I would say I am a child of God and I do teaching for him. But the teaching is not my identity; you could take that away and I still know who I am because it is not my basic identity. If I ask you what you do and you say, "Well, I'm a computer operator," that is not your identity; that is not who you are. But in a working world it has become that: it is our value to society that we do that job.

If we are not careful, that has become our identity and our fulfilment for personality. Those are the people who go to pieces quickly after they retire because they don't know who they are when they retire. They have been a butcher, a baker, a candlestick maker and now they are not, and life has lost its identity for them. That is where Christians have the advantage every time. Who we are is not what we *do*. It is right that we do work, but it is not our identity.

The fourth result of the Fall is that work invariably has become a means to an end outside itself. It doesn't have value in itself. It has value for another purpose, value for leisure primarily in our modern world. Most people regard life as something you do on the weekend. That is why we now have five-day weeks and two-day leisure, and not even one of those for God. But we demanded more leisure. We were not made for a five-day week.

If you live in Israel today you will work for six full days and you have one day off. That is the day when you will go to the synagogue if you are a religious Jew, but ninety percent of the Jews in Israel are secular Jews and don't do that except once or twice a year. But they are all on a six-day week, from the Prime Minister down. A five-day week is not biblical. Should Christians go on strike for a six-day week? I am just throwing that out, because to most Christians it sounds ridiculous – but really it's not.

We had a big campaign in England called "Keep Sunday Special" because the Sunday rest was being gradually eroded by many other activities. There is sport, but when it became shopping, and shops opened on Sunday, Christians rose up in horror and there was that national campaign. They lost the campaign and shops do open on Sunday, and Sunday is more and more like any other day of the week. We do miss the change and the rest that Sunday brings. It can bring the traffic down unless everybody gets their car out and goes off to the seaside. Sunday has radically changed, but that belongs to the old covenant so it shouldn't really worry Christians. But in the height of that campaign I naughtily wrote an article for a national magazine called "Keep Monday Special". I showed in it that Monday should be a special day for Christians. I will tell you why in a moment. But primarily because you go back to work, Monday is the most miserable day in many lives at home. Even for Christians it is: "Oh, another week of work starts." I suggested that all those who sing "Hallelujah" on Sunday should greet Monday morning with: "Hallelujah, it's Monday morning." I always use that on a Monday morning when I telephone someone. I say,

"It's Monday morning, Hallelujah." They wonder what on earth has got into me.

That article rather put a damper on the "Keep Sunday Special" organised by a Christian organisation called the Jubilee Movement. But I meant it, because work is to be redeemed, and those who redeem work can shout "Hallelujah, Monday morning!" I will come to that in a moment. In short, the Fall has damaged work ever since. It is one of the signs that the Fall has affected so much that our work has changed and made us live for leisure. Would you go to work if you weren't paid for it? There's a question! It is because we find work irksome that we are paid for it. We are given a financial incentive to go to work, and the assumption behind that is that if you were not paid you wouldn't work. There's something wrong with work ever since Adam fell.

So let us look at how work can be redeemed. In the name of Christ we can redeem our work and restore it to what God intended it to be, whatever work we do. I want to quote Martin Luther here. He said, "All work ranks the same with God," or, as I put it, "God is more interested in how you work than in what you do." I meet Christians who say: "I'm praying about what work I should do; I'm praying about a new job; I'm praying that God will guide me to the work that he wants me to do." None of them ever told me: "I'm praying for God's guidance as to how to do the job I've already got."

But God is more interested in how you work than in what you do. Unfortunately, the church has graded jobs for the eyes of Christians, and right at the top the best job in God's sight is to become a missionary. If you do, you will get your photograph in the church magazine or even up in the church porch. I was brought up on this scale of jobs at which the missionary was right at the top. Pastors and evangelists came a good second. Doctors and nurses usually came then, and teachers of children after that. If we are not careful we grow up with this grading of work.

Many Christians say to me, "I'm in a secular job." I say to them immediately, "Is the job sinful?" They say, "Oh, no." I say, "Then it's not secular. There is nothing secular except sin. Every other job can be used for the Lord." Now of course, if you are in a job that is illegal or immoral then a Christian's duty is to get out of that as soon as possible. I remember vividly a lady who came to our church for the first time. She could have been anything. Since we kindly left the front rows for visitors she walked right down the church to the front to find a seat. She walked down the aisle like a mannequin parade. I can still see the vivid turquoise clothes – I just noticed the colour. All the ladies of the church noticed everything else about her dress, and she floated down the aisle to the front and sat down. She was perfectly dressed. I think everybody wondered who she was and what she was – her first time in church. So I greeted her after the service. She came for a few weeks and then professed faith and became a good Christian. Her name was Betty. Shortly after that, Betty came to me and said, "Should a Christian be in my job?" I had never asked her what she was; I was more interested in her as a person – as her identity.

Now she said, "Should a Christian be in my job?" – and that set my imagination in all kinds of directions, and I wondered what on earth this superb lady could be doing. She gave me a very surprising answer. She said, "I'm an owner of a large betting shop." We have gambling shops in Britain and this one was in Aldershot, which is the home of the British Army. Imagine having a betting shop in the home of the British Army when they get paid every Friday night. They came straight from getting their pay to the gambling shop and she would take their money. She said, "It's a very profitable business. I'm doing so well at it." But she said,

"Should a Christian be in a betting shop and own it?" I did not say no. I did not say Hezekiah 3:16 forbids Christians to own betting shops. I have often used that "verse", but of course it's not in the Bible! But I said, "No, I'm not going to tell you. I want you, next Friday night, to take Jesus with you into the betting shop and show him what you do. Then at the end of the evening ask him how he feels." She thought it a rather surprising solution. But she did. The next Friday evening she said, "Jesus, you come and stand by me at the counter of the gambling shop and then tell me how you feel."

There she was, taking in all the money, raking it in, and then she asked him how he felt and he didn't like it. She said, "Do you know, even though we made a lot of money, we can't balance the books. We tried, but something's gone wrong with the finance and we can't get the books straightened for this week." She came to church Sunday morning and she said, "I'm giving up the shop." I replied, "What are you going to do?" She said, "I'll buy a teashop, a small restaurant, because I've always wanted to do that – I'm going do that." So Betty to this day is down in Devon, the southwest county where everybody likes cream teas, and she is serving cream teas in a tea shop.

I have often given that kind of advice. I think of a young man who came to me and said, "Should a Christian go to the cinema every Sunday evening?" I said, "Why? Do you?" He said, "Yes, I come to church Sunday morning and I go to the cinema every Sunday evening, it's my habit. It was my habit before I became a Christian, now I've added Sunday morning service, but I still go to the cinema as I always did." I said, "Do you go whatever is on the screen?" He said, "Yes, I just go. It's my recreation, my leisure activity. Should I?"

I nearly said "Hezekiah 3:16 forbids that" – but I didn't. I said to him, "Take Jesus with you next Sunday night and see if he enjoys the film."

Well, next Sunday night he went to our local cinema, went to the box office, put money on the counter and said to the girl, "Two tickets please," and he happened to be standing on his own.

She said, "Is your girlfriend joining you?"

He replied, "No, it's alright, just give me two tickets."

"Well, have you got a friend joining you?"

"No," he said, "I haven't. Please, I've given you the money, give me two tickets."

Well, she panicked. She thought he was crazy so she picked up the telephone and rang for the manager who came down and said, "What's the trouble?"

"Well, he wants two tickets."

Then the manager said, "Well, give him two tickets, what's wrong with that?"

Because she had asked him who the other ticket was for and he had said "Jesus", now she said, "He wants one for Jesus."

Now the manager panicked and didn't know what to say or do. He said, "Well, if he's willing to pay, give him them."

So he went into the cinema and said, "You sit there, Jesus, I'll sit here." The film came on and it was not a very good film and he came out after ten minutes.

There is nothing wrong with going to the cinema on a Sunday evening unless it is something that Jesus wouldn't enjoy. The young man learned from that and he has never looked back. It is a very simple way. Now if the scripture had said, "Christians mustn't go to the cinema on Sundays," I would have quoted it. But the Bible doesn't say that.

In matters where the Bible is clear we should live by the Word of God. In matters where it is not clear – and there are many things that are not clear in the Bible (you don't find the answer to every problem) that is where you have to "take Jesus with you". Of course, when you become more knowledgeable about things you talk about taking the Holy

Spirit with you and asking him to guide you.

Well now, back to redeeming work, taking Jesus with you into work – taking the Holy Spirit with you into work. If you have already been filled with the Spirit you can't do anything else because he is living in you and will be there the whole time. How then do Christians redeem work? By doing it for the reasons which the Bible tells you. There are three reasons for going to work on a Monday morning to make that work part of the kingdom of God. Number one – very practical – you go to work to earn money to support yourself, those who depend on you, and still to have enough to give away to those less fortunate than you are. That is the clear, first reason for working as a Christian for the kingdom. It is right to earn money, to earn enough not just to keep you going, but to keep your family going and any dependants you have.

Still your ambition should be to have enough left over to give to the poor. That is taught in so many places that I can say it quite dogmatically. It is not right for a Christian to be begging from others. That is not a Christian calling unless it is absolutely necessary. That is why I am personally very unhappy about some of our youth missionary movements that teach young people – fit young people – to go around friends and relatives asking for support so that they can go off to a training course or off to be a missionary somewhere. I believe that is wrong.

When I had the opportunity to go and teach some of them in a discipleship course I taught them some of what I am teaching now. I said, "Get a job. Earn your money. You're able-bodied, you're able-minded, you have no excuse for not earning money for yourself." I quoted a text from Thessalonians which says, "Make it your ambition to be dependent on nobody." I believe that includes if you know you are going to retire making provision for a pension so that you have earned enough during your working life not to depend on anybody else after you retire.

Now these are very practical matters. Some Christians have felt guilty building up a pension for themselves, but that is providing so you will not depend on anybody else. You can leave what pension remains (if it is still eligible) to somebody else when you die, if you can. But I think it is right to have that ambition. I am not going to beg from anybody ever if I can avoid it. Now of course if circumstances change and you can't avoid it, that's a different matter. But an able-bodied person should follow that text through.

When my daughter died she had done more for the kingdom in thirty-six years than most people in double that. We only found out after she died how much kingdom work she had done for other people: in her daily work; as a teacher. She had been deserted by her husband the youth leader when her first baby was only three months old. She had to provide for the baby, for herself, and she was still supporting orphans in Haiti and she was supporting a missionary in New Guinea, a missionary aviation pilot. We had no idea, and she never asked us for a penny, and she was giving to so many people.

When I found her Bible there was one verse underlined in ink: Make it your ambition to be dependent on nobody. I'll share this with you. I thought the world of her, but I wondered what the Lord thought about her. As I was thinking about what I should say at her funeral I said, "Lord, what was your opinion of my daughter, what did you think of her?" He said this: "She was one of my successes." It is on her tombstone, "One of the Lord's successes." I spoke on that at the funeral and said, "Would the Lord have to say of you, 'One of my failures'?" That's all he said, but for me that was good enough to go on her gravestone.

Well, there is nothing wrong with earning your living, there is everything right with it. Your dependants sometimes include aged parents. Jesus said one of his sharpest words to people who were giving money to the temple whilst neglecting aged parents, and were telling those parents, "This is corban, this is for the Lord." Jesus came down heavily on that. Paul was equally sharp when he said, "A Christian who does not provide for his own household is worse than an unbeliever." That's tough talk.

Then for the poor, Paul says in Ephesians, "Let him who steals steal no more that he may have money to give to the poor." There it is again. All that is redeeming work, it is earning for yourself, your dependants and the poor. That is a big enough motive to go to work. The second reason for redeeming work is that through it you are serving other people. If it is a necessary task that is meeting other people's needs then it is loving your neighbour.

Therefore on Monday morning you could say, "I'm off to love my neighbour," and that is the work of the kingdom. "Hallelujah, it's Monday morning, I'm off to love my neighbour." Did you ever see your work as loving your neighbour? It's practical, it's meeting their need, it's *agape*. It is exactly what the Lord said when he gave us the second commandment, "You shall love the Lord your God with all your heart and soul and mind and strength, but you should love your neighbour as yourself." That doesn't mean in your leisure time running in next door with a meal for someone who's sick, it means your daily work. If that is meeting a genuine need, then working with all your heart and soul and strength from Monday to Friday is loving your neighbour, and that is a big enough motive to go to work, and to do so gladly. There is no hierarchy of service in the kingdom. Whether you are a taxi driver or a missionary, God would rather have a good taxi driver than a bad missionary, dare I say it. He is more interested in how you work than in what you do.

Let's really get hold of that and not make missionaries the focus of all our interest and support. And neglect the fact that there may be a member of your church who is the only Christian in the office where they work or in the factory where they work. They are on the front line of the kingdom and they deserve as much support and prayer and interest of the rest of the church as the missionary you sent to Africa. Having visited many missionaries in their work, I have found out that many of them are in a far more Christian atmosphere than some of the church members at home – especially if they are working in a missionary school or a missionary hospital, they are surrounded by Christians. But here at home some Christians are on their own.

I remember a girl coming to me and saying, "Isn't it wonderful, I'm changing jobs. I have been the only Christian at work and I saw an advertisement in a Christian magazine advertising for a Christian secretary. I've applied for it and been accepted and I'm changing jobs." She thought I would be excited and she saw my face fall. She said, "What's wrong?"

I replied, "You were the only person who could present Christ in the office where you worked and now they are shut off from Christ; you've left." Worse still, I'm afraid I must tell you that working with Christians isn't heaven. It was not long before she regretted moving. There's a little poem like that: "To work above with saints I love, that will be glory. To work below with saints I know, that's another story." Christians are not perfect. Firms that are filled with Christians are not perfect firms to work for. So let us not fall into that trap.

I have a dear friend in Australia who is known throughout that country as an honest second-hand car dealer. He was converted through recordings of my talks, and is a great saint of God. He sells a second-hand car every fifty seconds every Tuesday and Thursday. He is in big business. He's taken over an aircraft hangar with an asbestos roof, which I'll come to later, and in it he can get 250 second-hand cars.

There he is, two days a week selling them. When he was converted, he announced to the dealers who came to buy them, "From now on I will be honest and I'll tell you the truth about every car I sell." The first car came. He said, "It looks good on the outside, but," he said, "I wouldn't touch it." He says, "The chassis has gone and there's rust here." Well, they didn't believe him so they bought it – and he became a multi-millionaire because he was recommended all over Australia. He'll be honest about the car he sells to you.

That was only the beginning. Now at one stage he was out on the streets of Brisbane rescuing drunkards in his spare time. A national Christian magazine sent a reporter to report on this millionaire rescuing drunkards, which of course makes a good story. The reporter arrived at the hangar, met one of his employees and asked, "Where can I find him? I want to meet him and interview him?" The employee told him where his office was – in the most blue language you can imagine.

Every other word was blasphemous or a swear word, and the reporter got up into the office and said, "I'm astonished. I thought this was a Christian firm and one of your employees really let me have an earful of the most dreadful language."

My car dealer friend said to him, "Oh no, if any of my staff becomes a Christian I give them the sack, I fire them." The reporter was astonished and asked why. He said, "How can I be a Christian witness at work if I'm surrounded by Christians? Whenever one of my employees becomes a Christian I give him his notice and I find him work in another car saleroom where he can be a witness to the Lord Jesus."

I must tell you a little more about him, because if ever a man used his work for the kingdom he does, selling cars for the kingdom. A lady wheeled a pram into a big shed one day and there was a little girl in the pram with a huge head. She had hydrocephalus, water on the brain. She had been born like that. This woman said, "I've heard you're a Christian, would you pray for my little girl?" He laid his hands on the little girl and he said, "Lord, I've never done this before. I don't know how to do it, but I believe you can heal, so will you heal this little girl?" I have played with that little girl. She is perfectly normal, and it was the result of his prayer.

He is now called to heal the diseases that attack poultry and vineyards. The worst thing that can happen to hens is called "fowl disease". He went to a poultry farm owned by a Christian where fowl diseases came in. When that comes in you have got to destroy the whole flock and clean the place up and get rid of it. It is like foot and mouth. He went up and down those poultry cages. It had only just been discovered, and he exclaimed in a loud voice, "Jesus! This is your farm! Fowl pest, I tell you in the name of Jesus get off this farm, it belongs to Jesus!"

The next morning the officials came to destroy the flock, but they were perfectly healthy. He has healed orchards. I have eaten apples from orchards that he has healed and I have eaten the grapes that are bigger and juicier in vineyards he has healed. He has actually distributed millions of my tapes and done so much good. He is not theologically literate, but he believes. If ever a man did his work for his contribution to the kingdom of God on earth, that was him.

One time I got off the plane at Brisbane and he met me. He ran quite a big car and we drove some miles in it and it went at twenty-nine miles an hour in the town – and it had a big engine. It went at forty-nine miles an hour when we left the city. I couldn't help noticing that. I said, "Peter, you've got an unusual car here, you could be doing eighty and ninety in it easily." He replied, "The speed limit in Australia is thirty in the town and fifty in the country." Even when we were hundreds of miles from the nearest policeman that big car still only did forty-nine and I couldn't help commenting on that. He said, "But those rules were made for my safety, how can I claim angels to guard me if I'm breaking those rules?" There was no answer to that. He is just a very ordinary Christian man, and he is the most extraordinary man I have ever met in Australia. It is a joy to meet him. That is work for the kingdom.

Once I got off the plane in Brisbane, got into his car and said to him, "The Lord has been speaking to me while I was flying here. Have you left selling cars?" He replied, "Yes, I have." I asked him, "Why?" He replied, "My church has told me that I ought to go into full-time Christian service. They think I should be an evangelist." I said, "You've lost your pulpit! An honest car dealer on an auctioneer's desk has one of the best pulpits in the world, and you've lost it." He said, "It's funny, but I haven't had any invitations to evangelise." I said, "Get back to selling cars!"

He is this kind of man: he looked up and said, "Right," and he went straight back and continued his mighty work for the Lord as a used car dealer. That is redeeming the work. It doesn't mean witnessing all the time, especially not witnessing at the expense of your boss's time – he has paid you to do the work, not to be an evangelist. It is wrong for you to be spending his time on it. Do it over coffee or on the break. Don't try and do it while you are working. You are busy for the boss and that is right. Some Christians think that they are only justified going to work if they preach to others there. They have missed it. Doing work to their best ability when the boss isn't looking as well as when the boss is looking is doing work for the kingdom.

The third thing I want to say is that work is to glorify the Lord – that they may see your good works and glorify your Father which is in heaven. There is a way of working that glorifies God. It sometimes may cost you your job, but it will gain the respect of the others that you will do nothing dishonest, that you can't be bribed, that you do your work faithfully, conscientiously, honestly, and even stay in late to complete a job that needs to be done. People who do their work for their real boss – who is not the boss, but the Lord Jesus – who have caught the vision of working for the Lord in their daily job, will glorify the Lord. Sooner or later people will notice the things they don't do as well as the things they do. If honesty is only the best policy it's not honesty. We are honest not because it pays, not because it's the best policy, but because we are now honest people and we are serving the Lord. Therefore, we remain honest.

To conclude, who are we working for? Christ. What are we working for? The future. Every day at work I am writing my CV, my reference for my future job. Because when Jesus comes back he is not coming back for two minutes and whisking us off to heaven, nor is he coming back for thirty-three years. He is coming back for a thousand years and he is going to rule the world and we are going to rule the world with him. For the first time the world will have a Christian government and we are just not ready for it. Do you know we can't even run the church properly and we are going to be running the world?

I believe that Jesus is not coming back to judge the world – that will come later. It will come, but he is coming back to rule it for very much longer than he was here the first time. We are going to share the government of the world with him. He will need a lot of helpers to do that. We are preparing for that now. We are not preparing for that on Sundays. We are preparing for it between Monday and Friday. That is what he is noticing. He wants to say to us, "Well done good and faithful servant! Enter into the joy of your Lord. I am going to put you in charge of ten cities." That is what he said, literally. There could be somebody reading this whom he will put in charge of Singapore.

I spoke like this in England and a man came up to me afterwards so excited. He said, "David, for the first time I can relate my job to the Lord." He had been in a full-time job but it never connected up with the Lord in his mind. I said, "What do you do?" He replied, "I'm de-polluting the rivers of England because they are getting very polluted and the fish are leaving, they just can't survive." He has cleaned up the River Thames in London, which years ago was simply a big sewer.

He said, "I've got salmon running up the Thames again." He said, "I never thought that had any connection with the Lord. When the Lord gets back he is going to need someone to de-pollute all the rivers. I want that job. Now I'm going to really do my best to clean up rivers because I want that job when he comes to rule." For the first time he saw a kingdom purpose in going to work on Monday morning and I was so excited.

That is what it is all about. We are working for the future; we are the people of tomorrow. It is for the future that we are living. We are preparing to take over this world when Jesus runs it and to help him to make it what God meant it to be in the beginning. If your gift is de-polluting rivers he can use that. The job I get when he is running things is directly related to how I do my job right now. Did you realise that every day from Monday to Friday you are writing your reference for your job when Jesus gets back?

I have said nothing about housewives, but if you are one then you have a job too. Billy Graham's wife had a notice above the kitchen sink, which read: "Divine services held here three times a day." She had got hold of it. She is dead now, but she really got hold of the fact that her daily work was preparing her for the kingdom that is coming. We are already in the kingdom as individuals, but one day that kingdom is to be manifest on a world scale. Every knee will bow and every tongue confess – they will have to – that Jesus is Lord to the glory of God the Father. When you will be running the world with Jesus, that gives a new purpose to your life. And beyond that there will be the new heaven and the new earth and that brand new universe for people whom God has made perfect who will not pollute it.

I have no doubt whatever there will be work in that new heaven and the new earth. It will be congenial work again. It will be work that is fulfilling and satisfying, but it will be work. Heaven is not a holiday camp nor an everlasting service; there will be work suited to you, a job that will depend on the job you are doing now. That is my message. That is how to make the work you do every week work for the kingdom of God. You can still serve the kingdom in your leisure time, but the satisfaction of spending most of your life working for the kingdom, whatever you do, just can't be beaten.

In fact, Jesus said you are a fool if you just work for yourself and try and get more business and build the business up. He said, "You fool, tonight your soul will be required of you."

"Work," he said, "for the night comes when no man can work." Work does not mean everybody becomes a preacher or a missionary. I would hate to be in a world in which everybody was like me and all doing the same job. Once I was talking to a hundred doctors (at a conference for doctors). I said, "You will all be out of a job in heaven," and one of them shouted back, "And so will you, David!" That put me in my place. Thank you for reading this.

ABOUT DAVID PAWSON

A speaker and author with uncompromising faithfulness to the Holy Scriptures, David brings clarity and a message of urgency to Christians to uncover hidden treasures in God's Word.

Born in England in 1930, David began his career with a degree in Agriculture from Durham University. When God intervened and called him to become a Minister, he completed an MA in Theology at Cambridge University and served as a Chaplain in the Royal Air Force for three years. He moved on to pastor several churches, including the Millmead Centre in Guildford, which became a model for many UK church leaders. In 1979, the Lord led him into an international ministry. His current itinerant ministry is predominantly to church leaders. David and his wife Enid currently reside in the county of Hampshire in the UK.

Over the years, he has written a large number of books, booklets, and daily reading notes. His extensive and very accessible overviews of the books of the Bible have been published and recorded in *Unlocking the Bible*. Millions of copies of his teachings have been distributed in more than 120 countries, providing a solid biblical foundation.

He is reputed to be the "most influential Western preacher in China" through the broadcast of his best-selling *Unlocking the Bible* series into every Chinese province by Good TV. In the UK, David's teachings are often broadcast on Revelation TV.

Countless believers worldwide have also benefited from his generous decision in 2011 to make available his extensive audio video teaching library free of charge at www.davidpawson.org and we have recently uploaded all of David's video to a dedicated channel on www.youtube.com

THE EXPLAINING SERIES
BIBLICAL TRUTHS SIMPLY EXPLAINED

If you have been blessed reading this book, there are more available in the series. Please register to download more booklets for free by visiting
www.explainingbiblicaltruth.global

Other booklets in the *Explaining* series will include:
The Amazing Story of Jesus
The Resurrection: *The Heart of Christianity*
Studying the Bible
Being Anointed and Filled with the Holy Spirit
New Testament Baptism
How to study a book of the Bible: Jude
The Key Steps to Becoming a Christian
What the Bible says about Money
What the Bible says about Work
Grace – *Undeserved Favour, Irresistible Force or Unconditional Forgiveness?*
Eternally secure? – *What the Bible says about being saved*
De-Greecing the Church – The impact of Greek thinking on Christian beliefs
Three texts often taken out of context: *Expounding the truth and exposing error*
The Trinity
The Truth about Christmas

They will also be avaiable to purchase as print copies from:
Amazon or **www.thebookdepository.com**

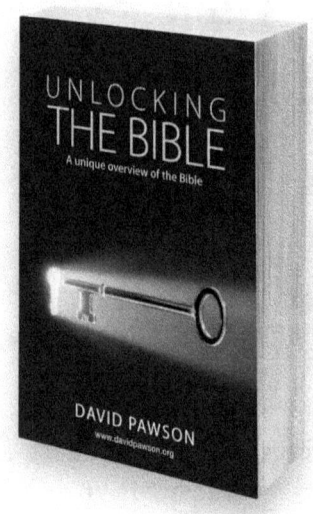

UNLOCKING THE BIBLE

A unique overview of both the Old and New Testaments, from internationally acclaimed evangelical speaker and author David Pawson. *Unlocking the Bible* opens up the Word of God in a fresh and powerful way. Avoiding the small detail of verse by verse studies, it sets out the epic story of God and his people in Israel. The culture, historical background and people are introduced and the teaching applied to the modern world. Eight volumes have been brought into one compact and easy to use guide to cover both the Old and New Testaments in one massive omnibus edition. *The Old Testament: The Maker's Instructions* (The five books of law); *A Land and A Kingdom* (Joshua, Judges, Ruth, 1&2 Samuel, 1&2 Kings); *Poems of Worship and Wisdom* (Psalms, Song of Solomon, Proverbs, Ecclesiastes, Job); *Decline and Fall of an Empire* (Isaiah, Jeremiah and other prophets); *The Struggle to Survive* (Chronicles and prophets of exile); *The New Testament: The Hinge of History* (Mathew, Mark, Luke, John and Acts); *The Thirteenth Apostle* (Paul and his letters); *Through Suffering to Glory* (Hebrews, the letters of James, Peter and Jude, the Book of Revelation). Already an international bestseller.

JESUS: THE SEVEN WONDERS OF HISTORY

This book is the result of a lifetime of telling 'the greatest story ever told' around the world. David re-told it to many hundreds of young people in Kansas City, USA, who heard it with uninhibited enthusiasm, 'tweeting' on the internet about 'this cute old English gentleman' even while he was speaking.

Taking the middle section of the Apostles' Creed as a framework, David explains the fundamental facts about Jesus on which the Christian faith is based in a fresh and stimulating way. Both old and new Christians will benefit from this 'back to basics' call and find themselves falling in love with their Lord all over again.

OTHER TEACHINGS
BY DAVID PAWSON

For the most up to date list of David's Books
go to: **www.davidpawsonbooks.com**

To purchase David's Teachings
go to: **www.davidpawson.com**

www.ingramcontent.com/pod-product-compliance
Lightning Source LLC
Chambersburg PA
CBHW071040080526
44587CB00015B/2706